Best of all, Christmas means a spirit of love, a time when the love of God and the love of our fellow men should prevail over all hatred and bitterness, a time when our thoughts and deeds and the spirit of our lives manifest the presence of God.

—George McDougall

Joy

For God so loved the world that he gave his one and only Son, that whoever believes in him shall not perish but have eternal life.

—John 3:16

Silent Night

Color Theory

It helps to understand some color theory when planning out a color scheme. There are three primary colors: yellow, red, and blue. You cannot make them from mixing other colors. If you mix two primary colors together, you get a secondary color (for example, yellow and red make orange). If you mix a secondary color with a primary color, you get a tertiary color.

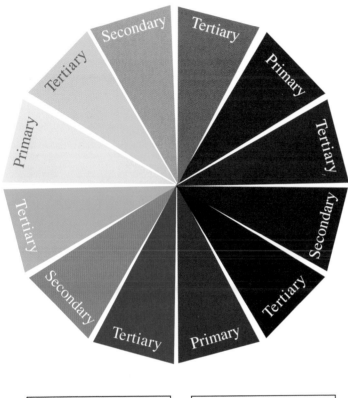

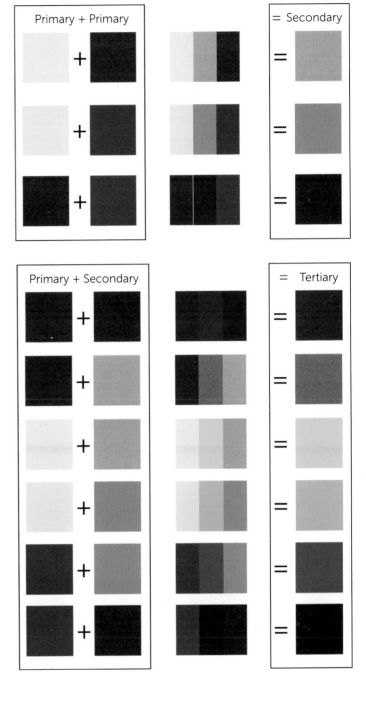

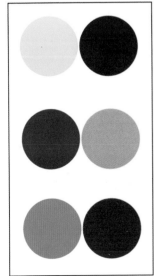

Complementary colors are opposite each other on the color wheel.

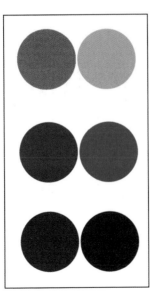

Analogous colors are next to each other on the color wheel.

The colors on one side of the color wheel are warm colors, and the colors on the other side are cool. You can make attractive color combinations by playing with analogous colors that are near each other on the color wheel and tell a warm or cool color story. Or you may want to have more contrast by using complementary colors, which are opposite each other on the color wheel and are a mix of cool and warm colors.

Holiday Color Combinations

When we think about Christmas, we think of red and green! But there are lots of color combinations that work well with the holidays, creating contrast, soothing harmony, dramatic impact, or joyful exuberance. Let's look at some possible combinations.

Red and Green: This is the most traditional of the holiday combinations and immediately telegraphs Christmas.

Red and Gold: Use metallics to add sparkle that brings to mind golden decorations and glittering lights.

Red, Orange, Pink, Green, Chartreuse, and Turquoise: Combinations that add in these tertiary colors have a more contemporary feel and fresh modern edge. Pink and turquoise are great for smaller accent colors.

Neutral Tones and Pastels: White and cream of snow and sugar, brown and gray from nature's birch trees and pinecones—these soft natural tones combine nicely with muted gold and silver and a pop of red berries. Pastel colors add a delicate tone.

Jewel Tones: Rich and deep, saturated and dramatic, jewel tones are regal and work great with red and green color schemes. They often include richer primary colors.

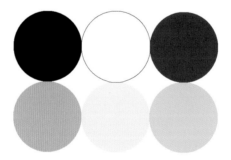

Black, White, and Gray: Feeling soft and quiet? Shades of grey with soft pastels are soothing and sweet. Bold black and white create a more intense contrast and drama and look great with some pops of bright colors like the classic red and green.

Warm or Cool Palettes: Sometimes an interesting color story is one that happens within a warm or cool palette. You can still find many shades and hues that suit the mood of a Christmas piece and make a strong color statement.

Color Moods

We create a mood in a piece by the colors we choose to work with. It's not that there is a right or wrong answer, just that there are many ways to approach the coloring of an image. You can create a lot of contrast, little contrast, single color stories, vibrant rich colors, or soothing pastels. The angels below

are colored in two different ways. I think of the right angel as more snowy, soft, and delicate, while the left angel is joyful, bright, and bold. Experiment with colors to see what combinations feel the best to you in your chosen illustration!

Color Stories

These two samples use either a warm or a cool palette for most of the composition. The red image is in warm, romantic tones of red, pink, orange, and yellow. In the blue image, I used shades of orange, pink, and yellow as accents—they are opposites on the color wheel from the cool shades, and I thought they added a good pop of color and interest so the piece is not too monochromatic.

These two samples use more neutrals, pastels, and black and white to create unique feels. I wanted to keep the background light on the first image. I played more with shading—which adds a lot of depth—and adding decorative dots to the bars and angel wings. In the black and white composition, there is a more dramatic feel created from the high contrast. I went back in with a white pencil (or white corrective ink pen) to add more lines for texture in the background bars.

Color Inspiration

The following pages are filled with colored samples to get you thinking and imagining. These gorgeous hand-colored pieces were done with a variety of different art mediums and by a variety of talented colorists. Enjoy the inspiration here before you sit down to color beautiful art yourself!

© Robin Pickens, www.robinpickens.com

Colored Pencils (Prismacolor). Color by Ranae Davidson.

Deck the Halls with BOUGHS OF HOLLY

Colored Pencils (Prismacolor). Color by Kate Lanphier.

Colored Pencils (Artist's Loft). Color by Kati Erney.

Watercolor Markers (Tombow), Colored Pencils (Prismacolor).
Color by Ranae Davidson.

Markers (Artist's Loft), Brush Markers (Koi by Sakura),
Colored Pencils (Crayola). Color by Llara Pazdan.

JOYOUS NOEL

Gel Pens (Sakura), Markers (Artist's Loft). Color by Melissa Younger.

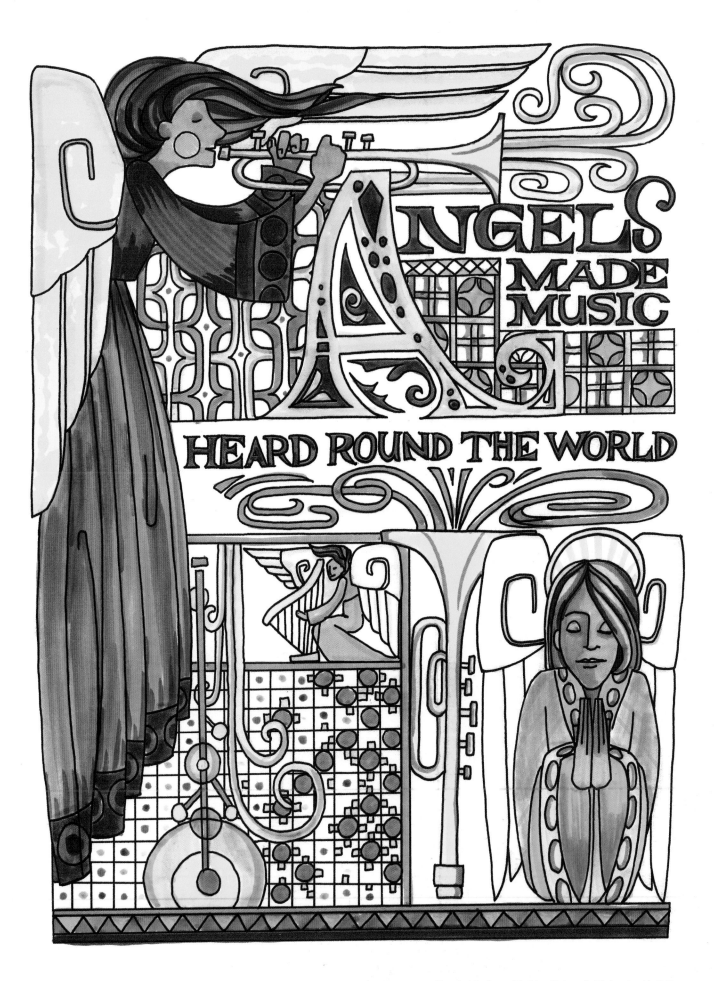

ANGELS MADE MUSIC HEARD ROUND THE WORLD

Brush Markers (Koi by Sakura). Color by Kati Erney.

Colored Pencils (Prismacolor). Color by Robin Pickens.

Colored Pencils (Crayola), Markers (Crayola). Color by Cindy Fahs.

Markers (Crayola), Watercolors (Crayola). Color by Cindy Fahs.

Merry Christmas

Gifts of time and love are surely the basic ingredients of a truly merry Christmas.

—Peg Bracken

Two Wreaths

When they saw the star, they rejoiced
exceedingly with great joy.

—Matthew 2:10

Three Wise Men

Hark! The Herald Angels sing
Glory to the newborn king

—Charles Wesley, *Hark! The Herald Angels Sing*

It's Christmas Day all over Earth
Let the bells ring out for Jesus' birth

—Dougie Campbell, *It's Christmas Day*

Bells

Christmas in Bethlehem. The ancient dream: a cold, clear night made brilliant by a glorious star, the smell of incense, shepherds and wise men falling to their knees in adoration of the sweet baby, the incarnation of perfect love.

—Lucinda Franks

It is the personal thoughtfulness, the warm
human awareness, the reaching out of the
self to one's fellow man that makes giving
worthy of the Christmas spirit.

—Isabel Currier

Bird Banners

And so, this Christmas season
May our hearts with gladness glow,
As we read the blessed story
That took place so long ago.

—Alpha L. Buntain, *The First Christmas*

Candles

It is Christmas in the heart that puts
Christmas in the air.

—W.T. Ellis

Christmas waves a magic wand over this world, and behold, everything is softer and more beautiful.

—Norman Vincent Peale

Chickadees

Share
the
Simple
pleasures
of this
moment

Christmas! 'Tis the season for kindling the
fire of hospitality in the hall, the genial fire
of charity in the heart.

—Washington Irving

Cookies

GLORY to GOD in the HIGHEST, and on EARTH PEACE, GOOD WILL toward men.

God rest you merry, Gentlemen,
Let nothing you dismay,
For Jesus Christ our Savior
Was born upon this Day

—God Rest You Merry, Gentlemen

Good news from heaven the angels bring,
Glad tidings to the earth they sing:
To us this day a child is given,
To crown us with the joy of heaven.

—Martin Luther, *Good News from Heaven the Angels Bring*

Hallelujah

Deck the Halls with BOUGHS OF HOLLY

Christmas is a day of meaning and
traditions, a special day spent in the warm
circle of family and friends.

—Margaret Thatcher

Holly Wreath

For to us a child is born, to us a son
is given... And he will be called Wonderful
Counselor, Mighty God, Everlasting Father,
Prince of Peace.

—Isaiah 9:6

Holy Family

The joy of brightening other lives,
bearing each others' burdens, easing
others' loads, and supplanting empty
hearts and lives with generous gifts
becomes for us the magic of Christmas.

—W.C. Jones

_____
_____
_____
_____
_____
_____
_____
_____

Horn

ILLUMINATE OUR WAY

Oh, forgive us, heavenly Father,
and help us to find the way
to understand each other
and live Christmas every day.

—Helen Steiner Rice, *A Prayer for Christmas Every Day*

Illuminate Our Way

Here is the message of the first Christmas and the message for us this Christmas: Don't be afraid... I bring you good tidings of great joy.

—Greg Laurie

Love came down at Christmas;
Love all lovely, love divine;
Love was born at Christmas,
Stars and angels gave the sign.

—Christina Rossetti, *Love Came Down at Christmas*

Angels and Star

© Robin Pickens, www.robinpickens.com

It's beginning to look a lot like Christmas;
Soon the bells will start,
And the thing that will make them ring
Is the carol that you sing
Right within your heart.

—Meredith Wilson, *It's Beginning to Look a Lot Like Christmas*

Mittens

Silent night, holy night
All is calm, all is bright
Round yon virgin mother and child
Holy infant, so tender and mild
Sleep in heavenly peace,
Sleep in heavenly peace

—Joseph Mohr, *Silent Night*

Nativity

And the angel said to them, "Fear not, for
behold, I bring you good news of great joy
that will be for all the people. For unto you
is born this day in the city of David a Savior,
who is Christ the Lord."

—Luke 2:10-11

Noel

The flow of blessings in our life is
directly related to our passing blessings
along to someone else.

—Thomas Kinkade

Partridge in a Pear Tree

I heard the bells on Christmas Day
Their old, familiar carols play,
And wild and sweet
The words repeat
Of peace on earth, good-will to men!

—Henry Wadsworth Longfellow, *Christmas Bells*

Peace Bird

The Season of Joy

Mankind is a great, an immense, family...
This is proved by what we feel in our
hearts at Christmas.

—Pope John XXIII

Poinsettias

Sweet bells they ring, they ring out the news today,
That Christ was born, was born on Christmas day,
Be near me, Lord Jesus, I ask Thee to stay
Close by me forever and love me, I pray

—Away in a Manger

Angel's Protection

UNTO YOU A CHILD IS BORN

O holy night! The stars are brightly shining,
It is the night of our dear Savior's birth.

—John Sullivan Dwight, *O Holy Night*

Shepherds

Share
the Spirit
of
merriment
and celebration
with the world!

I will honor Christmas in my heart,
and try to keep it all the year.

—Charles Dickens, *A Christmas Carol*

Christmas celebrates the awesome
and amazing fact that God is grander,
wiser, and more mysterious than we
could have ever imagined.

—Dan Schaeffer

_____
_____
_____
_____
_____
_____
_____
_____
_____

Triangle Trees

Remember that at Christmas time
A little child was born
To bring us love, from God above
A gift we should adorn.

—Judith Wibberley, *Just the Right Words*

Uplift Our Hearts

We saw His star when it rose and have
come to worship Him.

—Matthew 2:2

Violin